D1201506

Osip Emilievich

Mandelstam

An Essay in Antiphon

by Arthur A. Cohen

Ardis   Ann Arbor

Osip Emilievich Mandelstam

An Essay in Antiphon

Ardis Essay Series, No. 2

ISBN 0-88233-075-6 (cloth)
ISBN 0-88233-076-4 (paper)

Published by Ardis, 2901 Heatherway, Ann Arbor, Michigan 48104.

Contents

OSIP EMILIEVICH MANDELSTAM

AN ESSAY IN ANTIPHON

Osip Emilievich Mandelstam

I

It is customary in the recitation of Soviet doxologies for the voice to rise in clamor and alarm describing the Stalinist terror of the thirties and to soften with reminiscent warmth evoking the tremulous freedom and precarious adventurousness of the twenties. Occasionally, however, even the most official of official Soviets corrects the pitch of his voice as when the novelist Mikhail Sholokhov, condemning in horrific language the already convicted Yuli Daniel and Andrei Sinyavsky in 1966 blustered with rage that in the twenties "we should have known what to do with them."

The terror of the thirties, contained like a fist, was more haphazard in the twenties. Formal trial, public denunciations, self-incrimination, exile and execution were the way of the terror, but the twenties were no less comprehensive, although the means of that decade were superficially more spontaneous and disorderly. The condemned were shot quickly, the "counter-revolutionaries" were hunted down and put to the wall, the suspected were humiliated, deprived of employment, harassed from place to place, driven to madness or to suicide.

The year of the twenties which belongs to Osip Emilievich Mandelstam, the greatest and most difficult poet of modern Russia, was 1923. He was then a young man, just thirty-two, author of two books of poems, *Stone* (1913, 1916, 1923) and *Tristia* (1922, 1923) which had brought to him the most dangerous appreciations a totalitarian society can confer, celebrity and fame. Nineteen twenty-three was nonetheless the year in which the slow descent from notoriety to arrest, exile and death began. The portent of the year, missed by many, was not lost to Mandelstam. He missed few portents. He read the signs of the times accurately, but having read them, well in advance of those who would ultimately administer their official reading, he always chose to discern the ancient script of his Hebrew and Greek councillors, hidden beneath the block letters of doom. No less his activity in 1923.

It was in that year, having met Nikolai Bukharin, that he was asked by that eminent and highly placed Soviet ideologist to contribute a poem to *Izvestia* of which he was editor. The invitation, coming at a moment when Mandelstam's name was beginning to disappear from the newspapers and journals with which he had been previously associated, was a gesture of friendship on Bukharin's part, accompanied by the admonitory declaration that "it's important that you be seen to be with us." The poem which Mandelstam offered was hardly one which would satisfy the requirement. Short and structurally explicit, the poem evokes the rise of cathedrals out of the yeast-dough of the Eucharist and contrasts this mysterious transformation with the miserable "stepson of the Ages" who makes false bread and cheap words by the addition of a bit of yeast "to fatten dried-out loaves." [130].

The untitled poem, small in comparison with the major poems written later in the same year (numbers 135, 136, 137, 138, and 140, the famous "January 1, 1924") was nonetheless a glove dropped before the stone adversary. None picked up the gauntlet, but the glove was acknowledged in the mud. Mandelstam's public power had waned. He was not even able, some months earlier, to persuade Nikolai Berdyaev, serene sophiologist and acting head of the Writer's Union, to give the great Futurist poet, starving Khlebnikov, lodging because the one empty room under his authority had been promised to an unknown young writer. Mandelstam railed at Berdyaev with all the ferocity of "his Jewish temperament," but to no avail.

If Mandelstam could not secure Khlebnikov a room in 1922 he did not choose to hold on to his own in 1923. During the fall of that year, having managed a respite at a sanatorium in Gaspra, a popular Crimean spa, Mandelstam

received the visitation of a chronic provoca-
teur, Abram Efros, art historian and translator,
who informed him that in his absence the
directorate of Herzen House where the Mandelstams had a tiny apartment had censured his
coarseness for having requested less noise in
the hallways. Mandelstam immediately wrote
and improvidently rejected the authority of
the directorate and renounced his room. This
inaugurated what was to become the constant
of the closing period of his life, the "fantastic
homelessness" as Madame Mandelstam called
it, where traveling light, with little more than
the clothes on their backs and the bundles of
his papers and manuscripts, they moved from
house to house, apartment to apartment, room
to room, hallway, kitchen room, bed in the
house of friend, relative, stranger until at the
very end no place at all remained which was
their proper place. Nineteen twenty-three
marked the end of proper place.

But more than these—spiky clutchings of
the hawk, read in the sand as print of the
depredator, eyes alert, floating above—was
the composition of the tiny, emblematic essay,
Humanism and the Present which was pub-

13

lished, oddly enough in view of their later animosity, in Alexei Tolstoy's newspaper *On the Eve* in Berlin and the commission, writing and rejection of Mandelstam's prose memoir, *The Noise of Time.*

Mandelstam possessed as Victor Terras epitomized it "an 'absolute pitch' for time."[1] Most writers can evoke temporality, but it flees no less perceptibly, escaping nomenclature. Precisely, however, because time was for Mandelstam the rhythm of consciousness, it possessed weight, substance, dimension. Time and "the times" were both aspects of the poet's sense of duration. It is in this sense that *The Noise of Time* is characterized by an almost baroque counterpoint—images of domestic confusion, "Judaic chaos," ambiguity, rootlessness contrasted with *fin de siècle* Petersburg, its splendid gardens, glass railway stations, glorious concerts conducted before hysterical audiences of hierophants, operatic uniforms and spectacular parades, Italianate architecture amid Flemish ambiance and the tense expectancy of the young aristocrats of the Tenishev Academy where Mandelstam, and later Vladimir Nabokov, were edu-

14

cated, and the motley of poor, Poles, and Jews who coarsely bordered its silken constituency. *The Noise of Time* contains no chronology, but its pace is chronometric. It is as though time were the blood system and musculature of a chart of Vesalius; the internal connections were offered in high relief, but the skin of events, dates, ordinary movements are virtually ignored.[2]

The Noise of Time was surely no Marxist autobiography. Isay Lezhnev, the editor of *Russia (Rossiia)* who commissioned the memoir, declined it with the comment that it was hardly "what the age demanded." Moreover, as Madame Mandelstam observes ruefully, Lezhnev had written an alternate version of childhood reminiscence rather more acceptable, the story of the deprived Jewish lad growing up to embrace Marxism-Leninism. Nikolai Tikhonov, whom Clarence Brown acidly observes was one of the government's "most reliable utensils," also declined the manuscript.[3]

The fall of 1923, upon their return to Moscow, found Mandelstam's situation increasingly bleak. Within a half year virtually all of the journals of the nation had become closed to him. Bukharin told him "I cannot publish you—give me translations." Vladimir Narbut, a fellow poet from Acmeist days, and head of a major publishing house, told him the same thing. Mandelstam, along with Anna Akhmatova, had passed to the other side. It would appear that henceforth the only negotiation between the one and the other, between "theirs" and "ours" would be the indifferent plying of Charon on the murky Styx.

All this had become clear during the course of 1923. The poem "January 1, 1924 (140) written in Kiev at Christmas time ends:

> Will I ever betray to shameful gossip...
> the wondrous vow to the Fourth Estate
> and oaths solemn enough for tears?
>
> Who else will you kill? Who else will you glorify?
> What other lie will you dream up?
> There's the Underwood's cartilage: hurry, rip out a key,
> and you'll find a pike's small bone.
> And the deposit of lime in the sick son's blood
> will melt, and there'll be a burst of blessed laughter...
> But the typewriter's simple sonatina
> is only a shadow of those mighty sonatas.

16

The year concluded with a palpable shudder. It had commenced with one no less ominous. Withholding discussion of it until this moment, although mentioned earlier, is to indicate something of the Mandelstam essence, its quiet and unassuming heroism. The dramas of Mandelstam's life, his intercession on behalf of five unknown old men whose execution he singlehandedly averted, his interference with the assassin Bliumkin whose countersigned death warrants Mandelstam snatched and tore up before an astonished crowd, his later public slapping of Alexei Tolstoy after the latter's insulting behavior towards Madame Mandelstam, are not the actions of a public man. They are not the gestures of men who bend time to themselves, wearing it like their skin, acclimating truth and history to their requirements. There is nothing about Mandelstam which is sensible if the sense of his age is one of accommodation and complaisance.

I had thought, earlier in my reflections about Mandelstam that the opinion of Sidney Monas, whose suggestive essay introduces a translation of the poems of Mandelstam, was correct. Monas avers that Mandelstam was a

" 'Holy Fool'; a *iurodivyi* of seventeenth century Russia, a 'bird of God;' he was one of those imitators of Christ, God's fools, who were during Russia's times of trouble alone privileged to criticize the State." I have often dealt with Holy Fools, considering in that remarkable company Jehuda Halevi, St. Teresa of Avila, Ramon Lull, Antonio Gaudi, Miguel de Unamuno, but they are all Spaniards and the heat and wine of Spain make believing men of genius deranged by God. It is too simple a category. We cannot make the few heroes that we have Holy Fools—too easy to make them mini-divinities and saints if we believe them (and then dismiss them as impossible models) and incompetents, idiots, simple out-of-steps if we do not believe them (no less to dismiss them).

The instruction of Mandelstam is not that he was a Holy Fool, but that he was the only kind of man worth trying to be, and that even if he was alone (and he was not) and even if his witness was wasted (and it was not) and even if he was unique (and most assuredly he was) it is for all these reasons crucial that we not allow him to become simply the dead exemplum of hopeless folly.

Mandelstam was a witness, but not a holy fool. The point of the matter—and it is altogether clear in his work—is that Mandelstam was only what he understood poetry to require (and I might add, not poetry alone, but any talent which one believes is given to a man, not as an earned right and privilege, but as a gift on loan, including, lest it be forgotten, his life).

All this is clearly set forth by Mandelstam in the essay *Humanism and the Present* which was published on January 20, 1923. Undoubtedly a year later it would not have been published and would have perhaps been lost. It is a remarkable document, the theme of which is explicit in its opening words:

There are epochs which contend that they care nothing for man, that he is to be used like brick or cement, that he is to be built with, not for. Social architecture is measured by the scale of man. At times it becomes inimical to man and feeds its own grandeur on his debasement and nullity.

Assyrian prisoners swarm like baby chicks under the feet of a huge emperor; warriors, personifying the hostile might of government, kill bound pygmies with long spears; and Egyptians and Egyptian builders treat the human mass as a material of which there must be a sufficiency and which must be delivered in any desired quantity.

But there also exists a different social architecture of which man is also the scale and measure, but which builds for man rather than with him...[4]

A not unconvincing argument could be made that all of Mandelstam's principal themes and sources are compressed into this little essay—the scale of space and the rush of time, Biblical eternity and the historical juggernauts of Babylon and the Pharaohs (analogues to the juggernauts of the twentieth century), the social architecture that produced the Hagia Sophia, Notre Dame of Paris, the Admiralty building in Petersburg (about all of which Mandelstam wrote eloquent poems) and the architecture of an age which is built—like the Tatars before Moscow in the Middle Ages—upon mounds of human skulls and, finally, anticipating the sensuous detail, longing, and pain of *The Noise of Time,* his evocation of the innocence of the nineteenth century, which did not know whether the century being born was "the wing of approaching night or the shadow of our native city."

The essay closes with a complex image of values of humanism, out of circulation, concealed like gold currency which supports all the paper values of modern culture, all the more valuable for being hidden and latent. "The transition to gold currency is the business of the future, and we shall see the replacement of temporary ideas—paper notes—by the gold coinage of the European humanistic tradition, and the splendid florins of humanism will ring not against the archeologist's spade but in the light of their own day and, when the moment has come, will be the hard cash that passes from hand to hand."

Such an extraordinary image for humanism, but nonetheless a desperate image, for only a short time later Mandelstam was to conclude his poem "The Horseshoe Finder" (136) with these lines:

Some
        depict on their coins a lion,
Others—
        a head;
All kinds of copper, gold and bronze pieces

With identical honor lie on the earth.
The age, in trying to bite through them, leaves its
  toothmarks on them.

Time cuts me down like a coin,
And I'm no longer sufficient to myself.

Sadness enveloped Mandelstam like a fog, contesting his earlier conviction that man was the hardest thing in the world, instructing him that only some men were hard and that those hard ones would be tested and tested until they, too, crumbled, revealing the softness of all that is human, the skull for the city's foundations, the end of the old humanism and the triumph of the new architecture of the realists.

It is interesting that at the end of 1923 Mandelstam interviewed the young Annamese revolutionary leader Nguyen Ai Quoc, later to become known as Ho Chi Minh, for *Ogonek*. In that touching and lovely interview, strange beyond belief, if one considers the respondents and their fate, Mandelstam sees in the "nobility of manner and in the dim, soft voice of Nguyen Ai Quoc" the advent of a different tomorrow than either of them would behold, "the oceanic silence of universal brother-hood."[5]

This is all there was to 1923. Behind Mandelstam was fame and recognition, and before him would be harassment unto death. The curious fact, however, which Madame Mandelstam's memoirs of her husband and friend makes clear is that Mandelstam never wearied of life and, despite his desperate attempt at suicide in 1934, in Cherdyn, way-station of exile, his spirit throughout the long period of trial, arrest, exile, rearrest and murder was one of buoyancy and joy in all the detail of life— precisely the *detail* which makes the quotidian existence of many men unbearable saved his from utter despair.

Mandelstam remarked in 1921 that "just as a person does not choose his parents, a people does not choose its poets." The people of Russia did not choose Mandelstam and finally did not want him, but the insane fact is that Mandelstam perservered—nourished by small stones along the Black Sea, the narcissism of gold finches, the mysteries of crystallography, the delight in sweets, an occasional beefsteak, a fresh loaf of bread, the continuity

23

of friendship, the love of Nadezhda Mandelstam. What kept him alive and, for the main, productive, had to be something which most men of similar disposition and temperament would have found insufficient.

The issue for us—dealing with a figure of the genius and power of Osip Mandelstam—is how was it done? What enables some men to endure, beyond the predisposition of mysterious gene pools and the accidents of fortune while other men give over. Good men give over—Walter Benjamin comes to mind, desperate in Port Bou, or the great poet and admirer of Mandelstam, Paul Celan, suicide in Paris—but Mandelstam literally had to be dragged to his death, although there was precedent enough in his homeland—Esenin, Mayakovsky, Tsvetaeva—to anticipate the murderers with suicide. These are some of the questions I care about and wish to explore.

II

The St. Petersburg to which Osip Mandelstam was brought by his parents shortly after his birth in Warsaw in 1891 was inhospitable to Jews.

Imperial Russia, whose Jewish population exceeded five million persons, was segregated preponderantly to the Pale of Settlement surrounded by eighty-five million or more Russians who had been described a decade earlier, following the assassination of Tsar Alexander II, by a minister of state, Count Nikolai P. Ignatiev as "clamoring" for their expulsion. No wonder that the twin capitals of Russia, St. Petersburg and Moscow, should have among their populations few Jews, these principally Jews of wealth and utility, admitted to their precincts by special police permission. Curiously enough, in the very year in which Mandelstam was born, all the Jews of Moscow were expelled on the first day of Passover and their principal synagogue, newly built, closed and converted into a charitable institution.

It is remarkable that the Mandelstam family should have been granted permission to settle and remain in St. Petersburg. There is little indication in any of the sources—even the comprehensive memoirs of Madame Mandelstam—under whose protection (undoubtedly well-placed) was the Mandelstam removal from Warsaw to St. Petersburg arranged.

The Mandelstam name was of course known in Russia and many Mandelstams recur throughout the memoirs of Nadezhda, but none shed light on the quality of the immediate family. They are all namesakes—familiar with each other's history, clearly "talented," one a translator of the Hebrew Bible, another a famous Kievan ophthalmologist, yet another

26

the humble watchmaker in Yalta to whom the Mandelstams paid a visit in 1928 to fix an enameled watch and discovered that he was not only a Mandelstam but had compiled a comprehensive genealogical tree which reflected, it averred, an eminent rabbinical progenitor.

The family line of the Mandelstams ascends from roots sunk in Kurland, whither Biron, the duke of that Baltic province, had enticed them from Germany several centuries earlier. At the time of their removal from Germany to Kurland the Mandelstams still bore their ancient Hebrew name, but Madame Mandelstam could not recall it. She quite typically assumes that it was of a noble rabbinical line, but concludes her description by raising a critical eyebrow at Osip's fascination with his lineage. Having finished *The Noise of Time* and *The Egyptian Stamp,* a post-Gogolian fiction in which Mandelstam had appropriated Golyadkin, hero of Dostoevsky's *Double* as his ancestor, was quite sufficient genealogy for Madame Mandelstam. "Golyadkin certainly appealed to me more as an ancestor than M's father or his brother from Riga, let alone the Kurland watchmaker or the Kiev eye doctor."

The noble rabbinical line, an undocumented fantasy, is not an unusual conceit in the genealogies of the disaffected. How many Jewish writers and artists—alienated or ambivalent—recollect the misty rabbinical past as though the ancient tradition were virtual in their lives, sedimented and now precipitate in the new liquor of socialism, science, or Christianity. (The rabbinical origins of the Mandelstams—watchmaker and jeweler of Germany who knew Hebrew and Talmud, as everyone in a settled profession knew Scripture and its commentaries in those days—are perpetuated in the jacket copy of the Gallimard edition of Mandelstam's prose, where the author of *La Rage Littéraire* is described as having descended from "a father raised in the Talmudic tradition.") But Madame Mandelstam prefers Golyadkin. It is not quite as clear which Osip preferred. It is doubtful he would have made a choice. His sense of facts being what it was, he would have accepted both, fictionalizing the appropriation of Golyadkin, but keeping his Jewish forebears sequestered, minor and undistinguished as they most probably were.

The normal curiosity about Mandelstam's ancestors and his immediate family is never to be satisfied. The principal reason for this is Mandelstam's own lack of interest in his family. Dr. Aaron Steinberg who knew Mandelstam in Heidelberg during 1909-1910 once asked him whether the distinguished ophthalmologist was a relative and he replied: "I am not interested in my kinfolk." This dismissive hauteur was not unique. Other witnesses report that during their friendship with the young poet they were never invited to his home. The point is confusion and obscurity; purposeful obscurity, unintentional confusion.

Osip Mandelstam apparently had a systematic distaste for family, for the artificial fixities and atmosphere of family. It may well be the case that his father Emil Veniaminovich, leather merchant and specialist in suedes, was truculent and imperious, filled with philosophic schemes and accounting books, while his mother, Flora Osipovna Verblovskaya from Vilno, was musical, presumably delicate and cultivated, speaking a constricted but intelligent

29

Russian, that his brothers Shura—the vague and insubstantial—and Evgeny, the apparently foolish and venal brother were no companions to young Osip Emilievich. Osip's home, not remarkably, was the scene of unexplained angers and silences, his father (called by his household *barin*), often terminating family conversation by retrieving his teacup and disappearing into his study to work on his philosophical system, as he called it, or upon his German memoirs which unfortunately have not survived. It was not exactly the environment to which a mature poet would repair for sentimental refreshment. But then there was little sentiment in Mandelstam and no sentimentality.

The education of the home, restricted to his mother's enthusiasm for music and her shelf of Russian classics, was meager. Undoubtedly father Mandelstam would have loved to explain his philosophy to his sons, but they were apparently bored and disdainful and, judging from Madame Mandelstam's memoirs, not a little hostile towards that leather merchant and his speculative alarums. One suspects from the philosophic jargon preserved, in which quotations from Spinoza, Rousseau, Schiller, permutated in an alembic precipitate only to fool's gold, that Emil Veniaminovich was as Madame Mandelstam asserts, "the sort of person of whom one could not say whether he was good or bad, mean or generous, because the main thing about him was his quality of being totally abstract." The deism which he professed until his death was the little that survived his appointment to a rabbinical career in pursuit of which he was sent to Hamburg in his youth. There, in a familiar tradition of the Jewish *Aufklärung*, Schiller was read, concealed no doubt behind Talmudic folios and at the age of fourteen, already enlightened, young Emil fled to Berlin, abandoned religious Judaism and went over to Spinoza and suede.

It should not be imagined from all this that Mandelstam's childhood was tedium and dreariness. His household was one of of pretentious gentility and estrangement, dominated by the remote and somewhat pathetic father (to whom Mandelstam gave the most solicitous attention until his death) and a mother, music teacher and reader of

Russian classics, who arranged the governesses, the French lessons, the proper walks and recreations of her children. He sensed early and recorded vividly the disastrous sham which made his home a mockery, its combination of what he called contemptuously "Jewish conversations about business" and the gestures of his mother towards properly Russifying her children. Yiddish was never heard at home. Of that Mandelstam was certain. The Dreyfus affair was a constant topic of breakfast conversation and Esterhazy and Picquart were family nemeses. The children encountered the synagogue ("as if to a concert," Mandelstam observes) only once or twice in their life, although the celebrations of Rosh Hashana and Yom Kippur must have been sufficiently well impressed as to be recollected. And yet no mention of Passover at all in Mandelstam's prose and that lack underscores one's sense of the home. It is a constant in narrations of Jewish childhoods that families, assimilated to the point of self-extinction, preserve the guilt inspired by the great new year and the great fast, but have long ago dispatched the domesticity of the family festival of freedom. Families, however, like those of Isaac Babel, where religion is being strained into socialism and the Bund or Zionism have taken over the place evacuated by God, the family celebration of the Passover is retained, often stringently observed.

The point is that Mandelstam's recollections of the Jewishness of his home confirm a sense of alienage, distance, strangeness which approaches the incommensurable. The aroma of anti-Semitism, the familiar signals of Jewish self-hatred are abundant, but they must be placed in perspective. It is a Jewish convenience (and one not without historical motive and justice) to ignore any writer or thinker who regards Judaism, Jewish religion and culture, the Jewish people with ambivalence. An historical injustice of Jews towards their fellow Jews, I deny its relevance and truth. The anti-Semitism of Karl Marx (despite its exegesis by Isaac Deutscher, the best of its apologists) is simply not comparable to the love-hatred of the convert Heinrich Heine, the cool and uncomfortable objectivity of Freud, or the accurate registration of discomfort and unease of Mandelstam. Most specifically, Mandelstam was never given the opportunity of encountering any form of Jewish life which was not compromised, not already dessicated by earlier contempts and embarrassments, not already undermined and eroded by the quality of his home.

It is no wonder that Mandelstam in *The Noise of Time* should evince his own estrangement—an estrangement which by the years of his maturity had become a metaphysical principle—as "Judaic chaos." The very phrase, remarkable in its power, is of course mysterious. The chaos which chokes with confusion and disorder, the tumbled Hebrew books, the parade of religious teachers who came and went in sadness, the Synagogue services, top hats, mouthings to "His Imperial Majesty," the segregation of women, the grandmother with ritual wig, the ghetto of Riga where his paternal grandparents lived, constituted for Mandelstam the kingdom of shadows to which the Russian year stood in grand and formidable contrast. And yet Mandelstam came to know enough Bible—principally, one suspects, Genesis, Exodus, the Psalter, and the Major and Minor Prophets—to be aware that God

34

formed the world out of chaos, that indeed, the opening words of Scripture, later inseminated by Mandelstam with the Johannine *logos,* made chaos the first breath of order and, whether God's spirit breathed upon the chaos to create the universe or in fact inserted the word into chaos, the preexisting chaos was within God and out of himself God drew the universe.

Poetry and profound poetics (and Mandelstam had both) cannot help but being virtually kabbalistic, intuiting better than most the vision of Isaac Luria of Safed producing the world out of himself by contraction from it. The phrase "Judaic chaos" is pregnant. It is not dismissive but precisely evocative and it would be to miss the whole point of Mandelstam's tragic life and heroism to think that his designation of the religious emptiness of his home as "chaos," "Judaic chaos," in fact, is intended as simple derision.

Judaism and Jewish culture were consigned to the bottom shelf of the Mandelstam world, but the spiritual deprivation which this entailed was a deeply felt lack. In 1908, Mandelstam wrote to his teacher of literature at

35

the Tenishev Academy, V. V. Gippius that "having been brought up in a milieu where there was no religion (family and school), I have long striven toward religion hopelessly and platonically—but more and more consciously." Mandelstam grew to maturity chafing at his Jewish descent, chafing to the point of an inexcusable pragmatic conversion to Christianity (the Lutheran Church) in order to gain admission to university, but he would, later, at a critical point in his life, when he was subjected to an explicit anti-Semitic campaign in 1928, reassert his Jewish identity with passion and ferocity.

Mandelstam's blood was thick with the agglutinants of Jewish identity. His observations of his world, his abhorrence of violence, his almost physiological discomfort in the presence of the powerful and anger with manipulations of power he traced (Madame Mandelstam confirms it) to his Jewish rage for justice. The point was that his Jewish self was fashioned from the components of pride and presence among the beleaguered. Descended, as he once said, from "sheep breeders, patriarchs and kings" he elected to oppose the swinishness of those who would disbar him from an honorable livelihood, from the pursuit of his craft, from providing for those who depended upon him. He tried to flee the craft of writer, to earn his keep by doing other things, but he was trapped by his incompetence to be anything but a poet. When even that dignity was humiliated and he was accused in 1928 of plagiarism in a case trumped up to humiliate him, he wrote in the enraged *Fourth Prose:* "I insist that writerdom, as it has developed in Europe and above all in Russia, is incompatible with the honorable title of Jew, of which I am proud."

Mandelstam was a Jew by birth and preternature. But he did not know what it was to believe as a Jew and it must be acknowledged, that this condition of ignorance is one shared by many Jews, outside the Soviet Union. Mandelstam's situation was not really different—a generation earlier—than the numerous Jewish intellectuals whom Madame Mandelstam describes in *Hope Abandoned* as presently converting to Christianity.

During the 20s and early 30s, before Jewish (that is, Yiddish) culture was destroyed

37

in the Soviet Union, it was possible for a Jew to find ready access, if he was Yiddish-speaking or knew some Hebrew, into circles that were authentically Jewish. Unfortunately even then, Jews were a suspected national enclave.

The pre-Revolution emigration to Palestine had drained off some of the best secular socialist intellectuals of the Russian Jewish community. Those who remained had little prospect for growth and maturation. It became virtually impossible by the end of the 30s and certainly by the end of the 50s for Soviet Jews to nourish Jewishness, even the pale Jewishness of permissible folk culture. Obviously the Jewish religion which continues to exist in the Soviet Union, principally through the activities of the Lubavitch *hasidim,* would provide little resource for a thoroughly Russian Mandelstam or those other Jewish intellectuals seeking religion to whom Madame Mandelstam refers.

Judaism cannot survive without its literature and literature has to be printed to be transmitted and taught. Even in pre-Soviet times, the extent of Jewish religious publishing in the Russian language was modest and even that has come to an end. All Hebrew and Yiddish publishing is interdicted with the exception of an occasional token edition. How then should a Jewish seeker learn anything of Judaism except through Christianity, so to speak, on the way back. But it is also the case that religious espousal—and Christianity is the only available religious espousal in the Soviet Union which can function in this way—enables the believer to assume critical distance from the throttling atmosphere of Soviet intellectual and ideological conformism.[6]

Mandelstam's pride was never broken and that pride, authorized by ancestry, was confirmed by what he took to be the Hellenic tradition and the Christian humanism which had grown forth from the soil of ancient Judea. His Christianity, not at all dogmatic or confessional, was a means of holding himself aloof. It was thus, in the deepest sense, a device of self-preservation, un-mystagogic, without fanaticism, non-theological.

III

If not a Jew, then what? Russian? And what would that mean to Osip Mandelstam and was that possible, indeed, possible at all?

Russia was a permanent mystery to Mandelstam, an endless subject of contemplation and conjecture. But if Russia was not vast expanse of land, nor extraordinary congeries of peoples and languages and if it was not history—the arch of time, less critical in Mandelstam's thinking than the colonization of space—and if not her historical monuments, achievements, state religion and tsars, then what was it?

It was St. Petersburg; it was friends; and it was the Russian language. Of these three, clearly the last was preeminent. Even St. Petersburg, experienced in the disparate sensations of childhood, became hypostatic in *The Noise of Time, The Egyptian Stamp* and throughout the poetry, as a constellation of language.

St. Petersburg was Petropolis and as such an idea made flesh and when the flesh began to rot, Mandelstam vowed never to return there to live, preferring to wander. And friends, the friends of childhood set forth in all their complex exoticism and ambiguity in his record of fellow-students in the Tenishev Academy; and fellow-combatants and allies in the struggle to give birth to a Russian poetry which would supplant Symbolism and abort Futurism— his colleagues Nikolai Gumilev, the great Anna Akhmatova, and Marina Tsvetaeva, another major poet, who was responsible, Madame Mandelstam contends, for piercing the net which held Mandelstam prisoner to Petersburg and showed him the other Russia, the Russia of Moscow.

There is no generalized "Russian" Mandelstam any more than there would have been a generalized "Jewish," if Russian (and not Yiddish or Hebrew) had been the *optional* language of his poetry. A poet's nation is his language and unless one wills to become of no language or of several languages or to put on languages without fixity of place, the poet has no choice but to become the language he speaks and hopefully, if one is great in the use of the language, to change it as profoundly as one is changed. But language by itself is not nation, however much the experience of the people is transmitted through its unfolding, resonation, and echo. Language is abstract until it becomes one's own language and then it is possessed, most particularly. One can speak of Mandelstam's Russian, but it is more difficult—assuredly more difficult in the light of Mandelstam's life and reception in his country—to regard him as a poet of Russia, whatever his passion to tell a certain kind of human truth to Russia in her own language.

A man whose nation is his language is correctly, as Mandelstam regarded himself, a *raznochinets*—a member of that nineteenth century stratum of Russian intellectuals, without pride of aristocracy, without connections, without fixities of position which supply values and convictions like prepared food. Mandelstam took his oath to that Fourth Estate of intellectuals and honored it to his death.

Beyond his death the judgment of his fellow Russians would be that Mandelstam's poems were "a Jewish abscess on the pure body of Russian poetry."

IV

It is still virtually impossible—unless one's command of the Russian language is flawless and pliant—to speak intelligently of Mandelstam's poetry. Since I command no more Russian than the alphabet, I am disbarred from speaking of Mandelstam's poetry as such. Moreover, with the exception of the poems in translation, imbedded in Clarence Brown's biography of Mandelstam, the translations which have been appearing of Mandelstam's poetry strike me as "clipped coin"—not the Brown-Merwin *Selected Poems* nor the Raffel-Burago

44

Complete Poems nor the fragments by many hands which have been appearing from time to time these past years in the little magazines exhibit the sovereignty necessary to persuade the reader that he is hearing the whole poem, rather than a variant, or a half-choked voice. Someone not ensnared by the new cult of poetic translations out of prosodic trots will have to come forth with an ear for both Russian and English poetry, ideally a poet, but as well a poet who can reexperience not only the language but the poetic event.

Fortunately Mandelstam wrote magnificent prose about poetry—principally his essays, *The Morning of Acmeism* (1913, published in 1919), *On the Nature of the Word* (1922), *Storm and Stress* (1923), and *Talking About Dante* (published posthumously in 1967), and among others there is Madame Mandelstam's extraordinary essay about his poetic creativity, *Mozart and Salieri* (1973), and the continuous observation of his views of poetry and its instruction in her relentless and magnificent *Hope Abandoned* (1974). Obviously the remarks which follow will not illuminate the poems as such, but hopefully

45

they will shed light upon what Mandelstam understood to be the moral hermeneutics of poetry—the procedures of its production and its autonomous power to command the will and attention of the poet who made it.

It is obvious that Mandelstam had the power to stand fast to the end of his short life. It will be no less clear that he derived that power from his understanding of the process of making poetry and the investiture of the poem with the authority to hold the poet morally accountable to his creation.

One cannot help but be astonished by the station the poet occupies in Russia, not alone in its literature, but its life. Russian society has been ennobling and murdering its poets for three centuries, engineering their celebration and plotting their downfall. It is an incomparable tradition, Byzantine and Mongol, hieratic and wanton. It is hard to think of any other society that took its pulse by hearing the beat of its poets and then, determining its relative health or disease, congratulated the poet or destroyed him. Perhaps the apocalyptic presentiments of the Hebrew prophets (poets no less) suggest resemblance, for ancient

Israel responded to her prophets as dramatically as Russia has attended to her poets. It is no wonder, although the horror is not for that reason minimized, that Russia should have, in its Soviet moment, treated her poets with a profligacy and improvidence which makes the most baleful and paranoid of the Tsars seem responsible gentlemen by comparison. The legion of contemporary Soviet poets who have gone to grim and unserene deaths, hounded, starved, deranged, murdered is considerable. There are as yet only conjectural explanations for this phenomena of Russian history and they should not be elaborated further by idle speculations about the character of Russian civilization. What must be acknowledged, quite simply, is the fact. Osip Mandelstam at the time of his first arrest, ostensibly for the composition and private reading of a poem against Stalin (286) was a poet known for two modest collections of poems augmented by poems written during the 20s, a book of essays on poetry, a memoir of his childhood in St. Petersburg, a travel journal, and a hallucinant novella. By no means a large body of work and yet Mandelstam was recognized as a power in contemporary Russian letters by everyone among

47

the intelligentsia, conveniently situated in Russia's two principal cities. Moreover, Mandelstam had from his early twenties in Petersburg been associated with the poets who had sought to effect a removal of Russian poetry from the mystical indulgence of the Symbolists and the theatrical modernity of the Futurists. The movement of which Mandelstam, with Nikolai Gumilev, the first husband of Akhmatova, Sergei Gorodetsky, Akhmatova herself, and several others had founded has come to be known as Acmeism.

Movements always assist their least talented members to an identity. The great ones create the movement and exceed it, using the tenets they project more as modes of self-elucidation than as programmatic guidelines. No less the case in Mandelstam's definition of Acmeism. If Mandelstam was an outstanding Acmeist it is only because he was Acmeism, that is to say, "Mandelstamian."

In 1937, Akhmatova records that Mandelstam, living in exile in Voronezh, was asked to give a talk on Acmeism. "What he said ought not to be forgotten: 'I renounce neither the living nor the dead.' Asked to define Acmeism,

48

Mandelstam answered: 'A longing for world culture.' '' The first part of Akhmatova's recollection is an affirmation on Mandelstam's part that the continuity of Russian poetry and language is unbroken, that no links can be removed for reasons of political expediency, that Gumilev to whom Mandelstam's essay of 1922, *On the Nature of the Word,* was in effect dedicated, could never be forgotten, whatever the official view of his political culpability. Mandelstam never renounced anyone of excellence. But more decisive is the assertion that Acmeism was the longing for world culture, that is, for the continuity of tradition and values, or, as will be seen, the organicity of the Hellenic and Jewish Christian humanism.

The Morning of Acmeism, written in 1913, opens with a procedural disclaimer.[7] Mandelstam asserts that for an artist a worldview "is a tool and instrument, like a hammer in the hands of a stonemason.—The only thing which is real is the work itself." The "worldview" occupies the role of an idea and every poem of Mandelstam is informed by an idea. The idea pre-exists the poem; the poem however is not simply the enfleshment of the idea, but its reality. There is in Mandelstam's view a virtual inseparability between the wholeness of the idea and the language of the poem. If the idea is clear and contained, the language of the poetry is given; if the idea is inadequate or imprecise, language fails and the poem is aborted. Clearly the poem is an event in the sense in which, the philosopher Alfred North Whitehead understands it, that is, an organism, novel and irreplaceable, recognizable because of its structural resemblance to other events, but nonetheless a unique intersection of time and eternity. The event is a *durée* in Bergson's meaning—an inflation of an instant in the movement of time by a meaning which eternalizes it. Eternity and time intersect in the *logos;* time is spatialized by the eternal. The poetic event is a *durée,* a blinding beacon light which singles out and arrests one integer of the real, revealing the structure of the real, signalizing through the event something of the totality.

Mandelstam's understanding of *durée* is principally based upon the few works translated and available to him, notably *Evolution créatrice* (translated into Russian in 1909),

50

*Essai sur les données immediates de la con-
science* (translated in 1911) to which was
appended the very important *Introduction à
la Metaphysique,* and *Matière et mémoire*
(translated in 1911), although it is surely
possible that he read them in France during
his sojourn there. Be that as it may and whatever the direct familiarity with Bergson or its
mediation to him through the writings of
Shestov, Nicolas Losski, or L. Frank, Mandelstam introduces some novel inversions into
Bergson's thinking.[8]

Bergson was concerned to undermine the
familiar philosophic tradition which conceives
space and time as essentially similar in kind.
The source of this presumption of analogy
Bergson locates in language. "The terms which
designate time," he writes in the *Introduction
to Metaphysics,* "are borrowed from the
language of space. When we evoke time, it is
space which answers our call."[9] The intuition
of *durée* (duration)—pure, unadulterated inner
continuity, which has neither unity nor mul-
tiplicity, prevents the spatialization of time.
The use which Mandelstam makes of *durée*
is specifically relevant to the consciousness

which produces the material of poetry. Since it is consciousness which intuits and fecundates the *durée* (and for Bergson *durée* is the *seed-bed* of creativity), the intuition of duration was revelatory to a poet like Mandelstam. It explained to him the simultaneity of the disjunct, the ability of the imagination to hold an incredible contrariety of images in suspension at the same moment and to reveal them not in priority and succession, but in lingual immediacy. But duration is also a concept which contributes to our understanding of Mandelstam as an oral, bardic poet. If Mandelstam had been in the habit of composing on paper—rather than in his head—of seeing the poem serially, rather than compressing it in the oral-aural discourse which Madame Mandelstam describes in her quasi-mystical terminology as "secret hearing," it is unlikely that the Bergsonian notion would have registered as mightily. However, since Mandelstam's own psychology was one in which the eternity of duration was continuously inseminated with particular images (images which had no spatiality or temporality, but were simply unwritten words) the *durée* expressed to him a notion cherished in classic poetry—whether in Homer, Virgil, or the Psalmist—that poetic language issues from the deep wells of eternal life where there is no before and after, no past and no future, but everything is sustained in the eternal present.

The poem is a metaphysical event in that it is already, in its very facticity, something more. Like the mathematician to whom Mandelstam analogized poetic creation, the poet can also "raise a phenomenon to its tenth power." The poet condenses the enormous reality, piercing to its essence as though the burning of the sun were trained through the lense of the image. The poem is not symbolic, standing for and pointing to another than itself nor is it simply the rehearsal of the mundane. The poem is—although Mandelstam does not use the term—a cipher. The cipher is not a symbol. It is as real as the language is real, as immediate as its beat and rhythm, as direct as the commonness of the things and processes of nature, but it is cipher because all that it is adumbrates that which it condenses. The poem is a compression of the whole to the singular and remarkable.

It is the curious Mandelstamian use of Bergson's *durée,* the language of event, and the conception of words as building blocks which underscore Mandelstam's passion for architecture. In the course of a lecture on the nature of poetry given to Russian students in Heidelberg in 1910, Aaron Steinberg had quoted Verlaine's line *"de la musique avant toute chose* (music above all)," to which Mandelstam who was present had commented, in the words of Goethe, that more than music, poetry must be transformed into architecture, since architecture was *"eine erstarrte musick* (a frozen [motionless] music)." But Mandelstam, I think, means by the analogy of poetry to architecture not only the materiality of words, their building block character, but the architectonic of poetry, that is, language as structure. The poetic whole is formally implicit in the manner, but the artist's idea—his vision—pares away matter until it emerges. This Platonic usage is, however not a Platonism of ideality, but a rather more mystical understanding of consubstantiality—the highest shares substance with the most modest, the most exalted is drawn from the same matter as the most humble and lowly.

The poems about architecture or the imagery of the architectonic, present principally in Mandelstam's early poetry, seem to disappear in *Tristia* (1922) or in the later poems of the 20s and the last poems of Voronezh. But do they really disappear? I think not, but they are pressed through a different skein. There is something immensely elegant and exquisite about Mandelstam's early poems—not refined and effete, but balanced, ordered, contained, held in the suspension of the idea, like flakes in a globe. The later poems, filled with the prescience of his own death and the death of culture, appeal to a different structure, no less architectural, no less architectonic, and no less divine. The poems following the opening of the twenties turn not upon the artifacts of culture, the making and building of men, the quizzical, conditional hope that these artifacts will endure as memorials to the life of man and man's trace upon the earth, but center upon man himself.

In Mandelstam's lengthy essay of 1922, *On the Nature of the Word,* he offers a last gloss on Acmeism, arguing that the power of Acmeism was "the manly will (to create) a poetry and poetics in the center of which stood man." He goes on to say:

> The ideal of absolute manliness was prepared for by the style and the practical demands of our epoch. Everything has become heavier and more massive; therefore man also must become harder, since man must be the hardest thing on earth—he must be to it what the diamond is to glass. It is the conviction that man is harder than everything else in the world that makes for the hieratic, that is to say, the sacred character of poetry.[10]

The superficial sop to the new Soviet man is wrung out in the closing phrase. The hardness of man is precisely what must make a man stand firm, planted in the soil of his tradition, and of the values which are transmitted slowly, diligently, continuously from their ancient origins into the future. The Gothic in architecture, like counterpoint in Bach—two recurrent Mandelstamian allusions—are images of man's adamantine character. It is only later that this hardness ceases to be a call to the future but the only extant resource to which a besieged man can fall back. Mandelstam never shudders or whimpers even in despair. He preserves the manliness of man (the *vir* not the *homo* as Clarence Brown points out) until the end.

The fortitude of Mandelstam, the courage which holds out even against the vision of the apocalypse ("Poem on an Unknown Soldier" [326]) in which everything will be destroyed rests upon a religious certitude. The destruction, when it comes, is not the work of God. It is as though Mandelstam knew well and believed that the repentance of God before his own divine petulance in the days of the great flood may be trusted. God does not break his promise. Man breaks all of his, but not God. The flood of fire and ash which will consume man will be the work of men, not God, and the promise of God that he would cherish and restore the innocent dead is a portion of God's justice which—when all else crumbles—may be believed.

Mandelstam turned south to the Crimea, to Armenia, to the borderlands of ancient Christendom to find the succor of an historical *déjà vu*. He often sets himself back into the ancient days where the issues of the Hellenic-Christian world were clear, where merchants in the market talked of God with the same passion with which they argued over crops. In the ancient world there was no divide between the things of heaven and the things of earth. All that has vanished, although Mandelstam found traces in Armenia in 1921 *(Journey to Armenia)* and was continuously hunting through the rubble of the real for new tracings. It was very much to the point that his passion was for the evolutionary theories of Lamarck rather than Darwin, for geology and crystallography: all the morphological sciences are grounded in "eschatological presentiment." In the early poetry there were real achievements which contained *in nuce* the perfection of which human culture was possible, but later, towards the end, full of foreboding, he had to content himself with tracings, the record of tiny events in the universe which signal that all is not lost.

The eschatological presentiment, the search for tracings which would succor hope in the face of impending disaster, the prescience of his own death, clear and certain more than a decade before it occurred, suggest a lugubrious and melancholy cast to Mandelstam's work. This would be a false conclusion. It is notable, therefore, how many of the poems of the very last years, filled as they are with the unnerving perception of his own death, are nonetheless counterbalanced by poems of extraordinary joy. These poems, scarcely mentioning the promises of God or the help which Mandelstam felt extended toward him by the example of Jesus of Nazareth, are nevertheless finally absorbed by self-knowledge as poet which prefigures the promise of eternal life.

> Having deprived me of the oceans,
> And given my steps a barrier of coercing earth,
> What did you accomplish? Brilliant reasoning:
> You could not be able to take away my moving
>   lips. [307]

As Madame Mandelstam suggests, Mandelstam considered his death not as the romantics, an undeserved portion, but rather as the consummating celebration, the last triumph of a man. A man who is created in birth, who is granted grace by the gift of poetry, must approach death as a redemption. Mandelstam practiced at death, that is, " 'dies' by arresting the flow of time and then, after dwelling in the protracted moment wrested from it, returns to life." It is in this way that Mandelstam understood that a man's life is like the providence of God, creating, bestowing, redeeming. Working on a series of translations in late 1933 and early 1934, Mandelstam glossed a sonnet by Petrach as follows:

A thousand times a day, to my wonderment,
I have to die in fact,
And I am resurrected just as preternaturally.

V

Osip Mandelstam has been called a Christian poet. This judgment has been asserted by a wide variety of scholars of Russian poetry, from Sidney Monas no less than by the scholar George Ivask, who has devoted a considerable study to Mandelstam's Christian imagery. It is undoubtedly the conviction of Mandelstam's widow, Nadezhda Yakovlevna, assumed by her life and poetry as well as argued in numerous exegeses of Mandelstam.

It is not my intention to take issue with this assertion, but rather to put to it certain questions in modification of its declarative force. Clearly the question is of interest to those of Mandelstam's readers who are Christian, that is, believing Christians who participate in the sacramental life of their faith and express their vision of the world in the liturgical and dogmatic formulations by which historical Christianity has articulated its belief in Jesus as the Christ.

I presume that Christian readers of Osip Mandelstam are not merely interested in claiming him as yet one more among the unsaved who has been granted grace, but rather as one—a most remarkable genius and a most remarkable human being—who was able from the heights and the depths to give them instruction and, as well, courage. He is made Christian for them by his example, but even for them it is more than this which makes a man Christian, whatever his witness.

No less a cautionary word to Jewish readers of Mandelstam who are historically inured to the *odium theologicum* or, as it is sometimes called, less gently, the odors of Christian sanctity. For them, the temptation to dismiss Mandelstam precisely because his imagery is rich with Christian associations, references, echoes, allusions, is to lose contact with one who might well have instruction and meaning for their own messianic inquisitiveness, for those distinctive expectations which are not the founderings of Jewish pride, but the most exuberant and joyful hopes for a kingdom of God regnant of men and nations.

It is indeed the case that a poet, but no less a writer of prose, speaks only the language which enables him to tell the truth. If Mandelstam was bent upon the truth, as we have argued, he had no other choice but to speak its peculiar language. But the language of truth—that is truth which is effective and relevant to culture—must be a language with a received history, albeit sequestered, forgotten, buried, even humiliated and condemned. The language of truth which has paid the price to stay alive is precisely the language which needs speaking. When men cease to be men, slipping precipitously in savagery, the only language that can address them is the one that can—hope against hope—stay their savagery, quicken their remembrance of the forgotten and elicit the possibility of renewal.

63

It is my gloss of Mandelstam's Christianity that the imagery of the Bible, the Bible which moves from creation and the efflorescence of Israel, to the "becoming" of the Christian out of the paganic is the imagery which enabled Mandelstam to continue to speak, to renew after the silent years, to recommence poetic conversation with the nameless other whom he hoped would want him again, would save his poems, and would read them in the future. He had, as he contended, no contemporaries. The future alone was his contemporary, but it was also his hope. The exoteric language which bespoke the hope was undeniably Christian language although it was much besides.

The evidence is only the poetry and the prose. It is my view that Mandelstam's explicit religious language focuses upon one point and one point alone, the belief that the justice of God is signalled by the promise of resurrection, that the resurrection of Jesus (palpable in the symbology of the Eucharist and the liturgy of the Christian holy year) is the evidence that God's word is God's promise and that the word and promise of God are never traduced.

Agreed, but then no less our understanding that both contentions, although differently symbolized, are present within Jewish religion, are expressed in the Psalms which he knew well and are, whether Mandelstam knew this or not, repeatedly affirmed in the daily liturgy and the devotional literature of the Jews.

The point is that Mandelstam spoke the only language he knew to the only people who required that language from him. He lived out that language to the Russian people to his own death and he died, it must be underscored, as Nadezhda Mandelstam underscores it, the fate of Jews.

The suggestion argued by Leo Strauss in his essay "Persecution and the Art of Writing" "that oft times in Western history history philosophers and religious thinkers, possessed of a true teaching unacceptable to society and its rulers, adopted a covert language in order to speak truth but preserve themselves from persecution" is, in my reading of Mandelstam, reversed by him. The rule of conscience forbids covert language in concealment of the truth, but poetic language by its very nature allows the truth to be as grand as the poet creates it, knowing well that, alas, the reader is frequently ill-equipped for such grandeur and receives very much less.

The poet's form, the poet's idea is his exoteric speech, but the specific colligation of words, the shadowing of the image behind the hand of the idea supplies that inter-linear connection which joins the public form to the private conviction. The poet in such a view is always both exoteric and esoteric—always speaking in glossalia. But we must be careful when referring to glossalia. It is a term too reminiscent of the Holy Fool, the religious stammerer, the dissociative ecstatic. Indeed, what appears as glossalia—the speaking in tongues unknown and undecipherable may well be a speaking, so compressed, so charged, so very precise that without a conception of the formulaic premise of oral poetry,[12] the Mandelstamian genius may be missed.

Throughout his life Mandelstam composed in his head, walking in the streets, pacing his bedroom at night, continuously moving his lips and, as lip speakers will recognize, hearing what the lips whisper, foliating the idea with the imagery which enlarges it from intuition into poem. In *Stone,* a splendid, but more conventional book, the poems tend to be short, but each of them contains a verbal impasto, sharp and vivid. That first book is a rehearsal of repertoire, testing the possibilities and the perimeters. It is a composed volume. *Tristia,* marking a break, and the poems thereafter until his death constitute, however, a poetry drenched by obsessional themes. As the obsession condenses with the Wolf cycle or the Voronezh poems, curiously the language becomes even more selective, leaner, the budget of imagery constant and almost familiar.

The late poems are virtually all sung in the head. The thematic and ideational content tightens to an apocalyptic scream alternating with lyric outbursts which relieve the depressive profundis. The late Mandelstam is a poet who could not help but compose, however the task of conserving the poetry and transmitting it had already been given over totally to his wife.

The *Codex Vaticanus,* suggesting a hidden and now revealed text of some sacred scripture, is the name ironically used by Madame Mandelstam to describe the last group of her husband's poems. These poems precisely because they are created in the head and only later dictated are all internally related, not alone thematically but linguistically. All of them rely upon an armamentarium of images which are able to serve all of Mandelstam's poetic needs. They reflect a condensation and selection. Many images which function in the early poetry no longer appear or, if they do appear, have changed function and intentionality. The images, sedimented in his consciousness, have assumed the function of a formulaic deposit.

Mandelstam is to the *eschaton* what the Homeric bards were to the origins of our civilization. Those early singers employed formulaic devices and observed thematic continuities in order to preserve a tradition about the heroic beginnings of man; Mandelstam develops a formulaic imagery and observes obsessional continuities of theme to apostrophize the position of man before the end of his civilization. Each poem in the Voronezh cycle can be read by itself, identified alone, even written down and circulated, summoned out of memory by a fortunate hearer or reader, but the only way the whole cycle can be created or preserved is by the intimate awareness of their inter-connection, their mutual implicativeness, the urgency with which one poem commands the next, the way one poem often recapitulates and extends or restates its predecessor and pushes forward. It is my intuition—alas, constrained from confirmation by my ignorance of Russian—that Mandelstam created an oral cycle of poems, an eschatological epic, which was produced not, as in pre-literate society, as a means of transmitting the heroic origins of culture but as the defense of a man, already fleeing *into* the inescapable terror which would consume him, guarding sanity by the insistence that his last poems would be an epic song to the end of civilization as he had known and believed it.

It is clear why Soviet society and its rulers had no wish or capacity to celebrate Mandelstam's work, for Mandelstam was to the end of his life quintessentially beyond political use. Christian (and Jew), Jew (and Christian), Jew-Christian, Christocentric Jew, Judaizing Christian, Mandelstam succeeded in making the issues of separation and doctrinal enmity

69

of Judaism and Christianity irrelevant to the tragedy of the broken conscience which is Soviet man.

NOTES

1. Victor Terras, "The Time Philosophy of Osip Mandel'shtam," *Slavonic and East European Review*, XLVIII, 109 (July, 1969). Cited by Sidney Monas in his introduction to *Complete Poems of Osip Emilievitch Mandelstam,* translated by Burton Raffel and Alla Burago, Syracuse University Press, 1973, 15.

2. Another analogy to musical *dereglement* of time is Mandelstam's own evocation of Dante's *Comedy* as comparable to what would occur "if the halls of the Hermitage should suddenly go mad, if the paintings of all schools and masters should suddenly break loose from the nails, should fuse, intermingle, and fill the air of the rooms with futuristic howling and colors in violent agitation...." ("Talking About Dante," translated by Clarence Brown and Robert Hughes, *Delos,* No. 6, 104). But the source of this fusing of the senses, where time becomes music, poetry architecture, paintings the *Divine Comedy* is certainly not Rimbaudian, but the much older style of the mystics—I think of the love poems of St. Teresa of Avila and St. John of the Cross where the mystic before the inexpressible Godhead can only fasten the overwhelming *numen* by a purposeful confusion of the senses. God beheld is actually tasted, touched, heard. Cf. *infra* the discussion of Bergson's *durée* in Mandelstam.

3. Nikolai Tikhonov (1896-   ), Soviet poet influenced by Gumilev and Khlebnikov, was Secretary of the Union of Soviet Writers (1944-46) and well-adapted to the requirements of "socialist realism" in literature.

4. "Humanism and the Present," translated by Clarence Brown appears in full in his *Mandelstam,* Cambridge University Press, New York, 1973, 102-104.

5. "An Interview with Ho Chi Minh—1923," trans. by Clarence Brown, *Commentary,* August, 1967, 80-81; also Clarence Brown, *Mandelstam,* ibid, 108-110.

6. The reader is referred to Salo W. Baron, *The*

Russian Jew Under Tsars and Soviets, The Macmillan Company, New York, 1964; Zvi Y. Gitelman, *Jewish Nationality and Soviet Politics: The Jewish Sections of the CPSU, 1917-1930,* Princeton University Press, Princeton, 1973; William Korey, *The Soviet Cage: Anti-Semitism in Russia,* The Viking Press, New York, 1973.

7. "The Morning of Acmeism," translated by Clarence Brown appears in full in his *Mandelstam,* op. cit., 143-146; also, *Russian Literature Triquarterly,* No. 1, Fall, 1971, 150-53.

8. Vladimir Jankelevitch, *Henri Bergson,* Presses Universitaires de France, Paris, 1959, 298-99.

9. "Introduction I: Retrograde Movement of the True Growth of Truth," *The Creative Mind* by Henri Bergson, translated by Mabelle L. Andison, Philosophical Library, New York, 1946, 13.

10. "On the Nature of the Word," translated by Clarence Brown appears in his *Mandelstam,* op. cit., 153-157.

11. "Persecution and the Art of Writing," *Persecution and the Art of Writing,* The Free Press, Glencoe, Illinois, 1952, 22-37.

12. Much of this discussion is indebted to Albert B. Lord, *The Singer of Tales,* Harvard University Press, 1960.

Bibliographic Note

Where quotation marks without reference are used they are citations from Nadezhda Mandelstam's two works, *Hope Against Hope* (New York: Atheneum, 1970) and *Hope Abandoned* (New York: Atheneum, 1974). Numbers within brackets refer to the numeration of Mandelstam's poetry established in the three-volume Russian edition of Mandelstam edited by Gleb Struve and Boris Filippov, Osip Mandelstam, *Sobranie sochinenii (Collected Works),* 2nd revised edition (Washington: Inter-Language Literary Associates, 1967-69).

Clarence Brown of Princeton University, to whose biography I am indebted, has been virtually single-handedly responsible for the introduction of Mandelstam to English-speaking readers. His translations of Mandelstam's *The Noise of Time, Theodosia,* and *The Egyptian Stamp* appear in *The Prose of Osip Mandelstam* (Princeton, 1965) and he has published translations of Mandelstam's *The Fourth Prose (Hudson Review,* Spring 1970), *Journey to Armenia (Quarterly Review of Literature,* VIII, 3-4) and, with Robert Hughes, *Talking about Dante (Delos,* No. 6). Brown's biography—*Mandelstam* (Cambridge University Press, 1973)—contains numerous poems in translation, as well as the interview with Ho Chi Minh and Mandelstam's essays, *Humanism and the Present, The Morning of Acmeism,* and long sections from *On the Nature of the Word.* His translations of Mandelstam's verse with W. S. Merwin, *Selected Poems* (New York: Atheneum, 1974) is to be preferred to *The Complete Poetry of Osip Emilievich Mandelstam,* translated by Burton Raffel and Alla Burago (State University of New York Press, 1973), although the introduction, notes and addenda to the latter by Sidney Monas are valuable and suggestive.

Last, one must acknowledge the service to Russian letters presently being rendered by Ardis of Ann Arbor, which published Nadezhda Mandelstam's *Mozart and Salieri: An Essay on Osip Mandelstam and Poetic Creativity* (Ann Arbor, 1973, 2nd printing, 1974), translated by Robert McLean, and has made available in the seven volumes of *Russian Literature Triquarterly* which have appeared to date numerous critical essays by and about Mandelstam, as well as many translations of his poetry. Particular attention should be drawn to the first number of RLT which centers on Mandelstam and the Acmeists. It contains several essays by the progenitive Nikolai Gumilev and essays by Denis Mickiewicz on the important Petersburg journal, *Apollon,* and Boris Bukhshtab on "The Poetry of Mandelstam." The same issue contains translations of Mandelstam's *The Morning of Acmeism* and *Storm and Stress.* No. 6 of RLT has Mandelstam's essay *Some Notes on Poetry.*

OTHER RECENT BOOKS FROM ARDIS

Nadezhda Mandelstam, *Mozart and Salieri: An Essay on Osip Mandelstam and Poetic Creativity.* Cl. $6.95. P. $2.95.

Anna Akhmatova, *A Poem without a Hero.* Trans. Carl Proffer. Cl. $5.95. P. $2.25.

Andrei Platonov, *The Foundation Pit/Kotlovan.* Bi-lingual edition. English Trans. by T. P. Whitney. Preface by Joseph Brodsky. Cloth $10.00. Paper $3.95.

Alexander Pushkin, *Ruslan and Liudmila.* Trans. Walter Arndt. Cl. $8.95. P. $2.50.

Wings: Prose and Poetry by Mikhail Kuzmin. Trans. N. Granoien and M. Green. Cl. $6.95. P. $2.95.

Mikhail Zoshchenko, *Before Sunrise.* Trans. Gary Kern. First complete English translation. Cl. $12.95. P. $3.25.

Alexander Solzhenitsyn: An International Bibliography of Works by and about Him 1962-73. Comp. Donald Fiene. 2500 entires in 38 languages. Cloth $8.95. Paper $3.50.

Carl R. Proffer (ed.), *A Book of Things about Vladimir Nabokov.* Essays, analyses, reviews, annotations. Cl. $10.95. P. $3.50.

Mikhail Bakhtin, *Problems of Dostoevsky's Poetics.* Trans. W. Rotsel. Cl. $8.95. P. $3.95.

Life as Theater: Five Modern Plays by Nikolai Evreinov. Trans. Christopher Collins. Cl. $10.95. P. $3.95.

The Unpublished Dostoevsky: Diaries and Notebooks 1860-81. Volume 1. Cl. $7.95.